THIS BOOK BELONGS TO

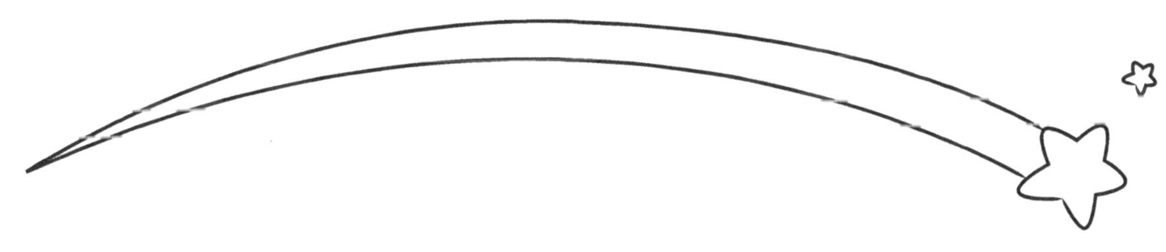

With love, I dedicate this book to Ashley, Brian, Ryan and Jake. May your dreams become more than just visions, your minds create goals, and your hearts lead the way to inner fulfillment.

Scott, I bestow upon you my gratitude for your resourceful "words" of wisdom.

Dreams are our thoughts transposed into vision.
They flow through our minds and our hearts unbidden.
For seconds, for minutes, even hours a day,
We see them and hear them while our minds play.

In our minds, it's amazing just what we can do.
With its power it can entertain me and you.
So what we call dreams, I'd like to explain.
Here are a few that I'll mention by name.

Daydreams exist, which are fun and daring.
Nightmares are known to be ugly and scary.
Recurring dreams, they happen at times.
And epic dreams, which are memories in time.

Then there are lucid dreams where we have power.
And healing dreams for when things go sour.
Signal dreams can make things come true.
In prophetic dreams, we the future may view.

Daydreams come and go as they please.
The images we see are just a tease.
They take us places we wish were real
And give us vibes we think we feel.

Daydreams can last from minutes to hours.
We picture stars, lakes, planets, and flowers.
We're happy to roam, both free and far,
In a world without harm, no danger to mar.

Nightmares are dreams that we may find scary,
With ghosts, goblins, or something hairy.
We'd even hear noises that sound rather creepy.
But, at the same time, we're just too sleepy.

Nightmares are strange and may seem frightening.
Our eyes will stay shut though our fists may be tightening.
When we awake as the sun starts to rise
The dream that seemed real was just a disguise.

Recurring dreams are ones that repeat,
Some places we've seen and people we meet.
The reasons behind them we may try to find.
Until we do, they just boggle the mind.

Recurring dreams are known to have meaning
In voices we're hearing and people we're seeing.
And if we are able to discern the problem,
We continue to dream and possibly solve them.

Epic dreams you'll find hard to ignore.
They're exciting and thrilling and far from a bore.
You could fly, you could soar, even travel in space.
There's excitement in dreams we could truly embrace.

Epic dreams are the dreams we hope never end.
These dreams we share with both family and friends.
In all the worlds we have seen in our dreams,
We see ourselves smiling as light brightly gleams.

Lucid dreams, those that are in our control,
Give us the freedom to continue our stroll.
Though there are times when we tremble and cower,
To face them and beat them, we have the power.

Lucid dreams are ones that build self-control.
They strengthen our minds, our hearts, and our soul.
Whatever our weakness, we can always recover
As long as we take charge under the covers.

Healing dreams happen when something is wrong.
It could be the flu, or our health isn't strong.
They let us know when to see dentist or doctor,
While our parents stand there to guide and to proctor.

Healing dreams are those beneficial to all
By telling our illness and then who to call.
They're harmless yet helpful to body and mind.
Recovery in dreams we are able to find.

Signal dreams are used to show and explain.
They interpret our problems, our issues, our pain.
Our decisions it narrows, and which ones to make.
They're great to help deal with what's really at stake.

JACKSON
DANCE
JACKSON AVE
CAT
FOUND!
JACKSON
TAXES
MISSING
CAT
238
LOST
CAT
FOUND
JACKSON
AVE

Signal dreams often are known to be rare,
But the mind can find in them much time to spare.
So consider the next dream and what it may say
As you're facing a problem, at work or at play.

Prophetic dreams, our future they foretell.
Though their meaning, at first, may not ring a bell.
Piecing together the visions and more
Tells us the future we have in store.

Prophetic dreams are put together
As our hearts rest on a pillow of feathers.
Never be afraid to interpret the dream.
They're not as frightening as they may seem.

So be happy when dreaming, that you get so much.
It's good that we're blessed by a dream's magic touch.
It gives us a new life beyond what is real
And gives us a new way to think and feel.

They come and they go at their own magic will.
They're happy, they're sad; they may give us a chill.
They can forecast the future or take us to Mars.
But as long as we dream, the future is ours!

Illustration by Toby Mikle

Published in the United States of America

ISBN: 9798695405521